A
Speller's
Companion

Fourth edition

Brown and Brown

Publishers: Brown and Brown,
Keeper's Cottage,
Westward,
Wigton
Cumbria CA7 8NQ
Tel. 016973 42915

First published 1987
Reprinted 1989

Second edition 1990
Reprinted 1991 (twice), 1992, 1993, 1995

Third edition 1997
Reprinted 1999, 2001, 2003

Fourth edition 2005

ISBN 1 904874 04 5

Printed by Reed's Ltd., Penrith, Cumbria on Corona recycled paper and Context Ivory recycled card.

Introduction

This book is mainly about words, where they come from and why they are spelt as they are.

The oddities of English spelling are well known to everyone who has to write the language. The reasons for them are not so well known, but they can be found by studying the history of English.

A Speller's Companion serves as an introduction to that history, and concentrates on answering some of the questions about words in everyday use which can be difficult to spell. Several exercises *(in shaded boxes)* are interspersed with the text to give some practical experience in thinking about how the English language works.

It is hoped that the book will encourage readers to look further for answers to their own particular questions. To that end, a list of books for further reading is included.

For this **Fourth edition** the text has been re-typeset and, where appropriate, revised and updated.

"In this work, when it shall be found that much is omitted, let it not be forgotten that much likewise is performed."

Dr. Samuel Johnson (1755)

(in the Preface to his Dictionary)

Contents

What is English ?

The English of today is not the same as the English of 50 years ago and it will have changed again by the middle of this century.

Language began as a means of spoken communication between people, and it has changed as people and their circumstances have changed. For thousands of years people led nomadic lives, following the animals they needed for food and clothing. It was only when they began to settle and cultivate the land that they found a use for a written form of their language, to record ownership of property and trading of goods.

It is from the written evidence that we can trace the development of the languages spoken in the British Isles into the English we speak now. The foundations of the English language were laid by the invasion and settlement of the British Isles over a period of about 1500 years between BC 400 and AD 1066:

BC

400	**Celts** (Northern France and the Netherlands)
350	**Celts** (Southern France)
55 - 54	**Romans** (Italy)

AD

43 - 410	**Romans** (Italy)
449	**Angles, Saxons and Jutes** (Denmark, Germany and Holland)
789	**Vikings** (Denmark and Norway)
1066	**Normans** (France)

Since then, English has travelled to almost all the countries of the world and it is now spoken and understood by over a billion people. It is often used, as Latin once was, as an 'international' or common language for communication between people of different countries when on official business or on holiday. English, in turn, has been enriched by 'borrowing' thousands of words from other countries.

In the course of time and travel, the pronunciation, spelling and meaning of many English words have changed several times over. In some, the pronunciation has changed beyond recognition, but the spelling has stayed the same for over 1000 years. Other words have been victims of fashion - French, Latin and Greek words have gone in and out of English over the years as often as hemlines have gone up and down. Some words have gone out of use altogether.

Many words have been round the world and back again. When the Pilgrim Fathers sailed for America in 1620, they would not have believed that future generations would decry the good English words (like *gotten*), which they took with them, as 'Americanisms' not fit to be used in the Queen's English !

English now has the largest and most varied vocabulary of any language in the world (and there are about 2700 of them). *The Oxford English Dictionary* has recorded over half a million words, and there are another half million scientific and technical terms not listed in the dictionary. In comparison, German has about 185,000 words and French about 100,000.

Until the present century, changes in the English language have taken place quite slowly - over hundreds of years. Today, modern technology has speeded up our means of communication. Radio, T.V., electronic equipment and computers now record the language as only writing did before. Future generations will not rely solely on the written word to find out about the English language of the 21st century.

But what matters now is the story so far - and how it affects the English we speak and write every day.

The Celts

The Celts were one of the many tribes living in Europe in the years before Christ. Their dialect belonged to a large family of languages, known as **Indo European**, which is the basis of the language of about a third of the world's population. It contains most of the European languages and spreads as far east as India *(see p.55)*.

About 400 years BC, the Celts began to leave Central Europe, possibly because of harassment from other tribes. The Celts from Northern France and the Netherlands crossed the Channel and settled in England, Wales and Scotland. The dialect of these people was **Brythonic**, and they were known as **Brythons** (now spelt *Britons*).

Later, about 350 BC, Celts from Southern France settled in Ireland. Their dialect was **Goidelic** (now spelt *Gaelic*).

Celtic place-names

The Celtic Britons gave us names for many natural features of the landscape and some man-made ones too. They can be found in place-names all over the British Isles. Some of them are:

cwm / cum / combe = a deep valley

lan / llan = church

pen = hill, heap, top

tre = homestead

dun / dum = hill or fort

bal = homestead, hamlet

afon / avon = river

aber = mouth of a river

> Look at a map of the British Isles and try to find place-names which contain these Celtic words.

You will notice that most of the Celtic British place-names appear more often in certain areas of Britain. The reason for this is that the Romans and the Anglo-Saxons, between them, drove the Britons to the far west and north of their country and changed all but a few of their original place-names in what eventually became England.

The Britons established kingdoms in Wales, in Cornwall and in Cumberland and South-West Scotland (jointly named the kingdom of Strathclyde). Some Britons sailed from Cornwall to North-West France and settled in what is now Brittany. Their language - **Breton** - is still spoken there.

At about the same time, Gaelic-speaking Celts from Northern Ireland crossed to Scotland and the Isle of Man. One of their tribes, the **Scotti**, gave Scotland its name.

Celtic writing

The Celts had their own system of writing down their language. It was called **Ogham**, after Ogma, who was thought to have invented it. It has been found as formal inscriptions on stone, mainly in Ireland and Wales.

Ogham letters were made with a series of straight lines, all stemming from a central vertical line. Although they worked well for formal carving on stone, they were awkward to use for everyday writing and, over a period of time, Celtic monks from Ireland spread the use of the Roman alphabet which included a cursive ('running') script more suitable for handwriting.

On the next page are the Celtic names of four English rivers in Ogham script, and a key to the Ogham system. Work out the Celtic names for the rivers, then pick out their modern English spelling from this list of English rivers named by the Celts:

Wye	Tees	Trent	Avon	Exe
Don	Esk	Ouse	Dee	Dart
Derwent	Severn		Humber	Thames

Celtic Oghams

Key

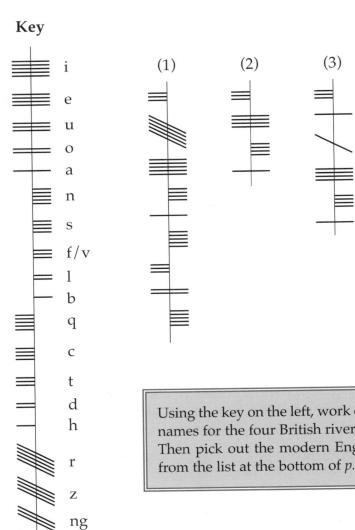

Using the key on the left, work out the Celtic names for the four British rivers above. Then pick out the modern English spelling from the list at the bottom of *p. 9.*

The Romans

After 300 years of calling the British Isles their own, the Celtic Britons were attacked and conquered by the Romans and **Britannia** (as the Romans named it) formed the north-west corner of the vast Roman Empire from AD 43 to 410.

The Romans stayed in Britain for almost 400 years and left behind them roads and buildings which can still be seen today, but they were unable, at this stage, to impose their language upon the Britons. The Britons continued to speak their Brythonic dialect, with only the odd word of Latin thrown in, until the next invasion of Britain began around 449. It was only later, when Christianity came to the British Isles, that Latin really began to make an impact on the English language.

The Angles, Saxons and Jutes

The Angles, Saxons and Jutes were tribes who belonged to the same Indo European language family as the Celts, but they spoke in a Germanic dialect which was very different in sound.

The Angles and Jutes came from Denmark and the Saxons came from the coast of Germany and Holland. They began to invade the British Isles in 449 and, over the next 300 years, they settled and gradually wiped out all traces of the Celtic Britons who fled west and north to Wales, Cornwall, Cumberland and South-West Scotland.

The Anglo-Saxons (as they became known) named their new country **Englaland** (*England*), and they and their language were called **Englisc** (*English*).

The Anglo-Saxons called the Britons **wealas** (which meant **foreigners** !) and it is from this name that we now have **Wales**. The Scottish Celts had their own name for the Anglo-Saxons - **Sassenachs**.

Anglo-Saxon place names

It is clear, from the thousands of place-names still used today, that the Anglo-Saxons were determined to have England for the English.

First, they divided England into 7 kingdoms:

Wessex (West Saxons)   **Sussex** (South Saxons)

Essex (East Saxons)   **Kent** (mainly Jutes)

East Anglia (mainly Angles)   **Mercia** (mainly Angles)

Northumbria (land north of the Humber - mainly Angles)

Next, they changed all the Celtic and Roman names into their own language, which is now called **Old English**. Only when they had no word of their own to fit, did they 'borrow' a Celtic or Roman one.

For instance, because they came from flat, marshy lands, they did not have words for some features of the more rugged British landscape, so they borrowed the Celtic words: **crag, tor** (high rock; hill) and **combe** (deep valley).

Sometimes they joined Old English words on to Celtic words to make new place-names. The name of the village of **Torpenhow** (Cumbria) comes from:

Tor   (Celtic = hill)

pen   (Celtic = hill)

hoh   (Old English = ridge, spur of a hill)

so, in Modern English, it could be **Hillhillhill** ! This place-name, like so many words in English, is not spelt as it is now spoken - if it were, it would look something like **Tropenner** !

Four Old English words which are found most often in place-names today are:

ham (homestead, village)   **ing** (follower of)

ton / **tun** (enclosure, village)   **wic** (dairy farm, camp)

Are any of them found often in your area - or are there other, more common, ones ?

Many British and Roman towns were built round a fort or castle which housed the army and, although the Anglo-Saxons re-named them all, they are easy to pick out on a map because the Old English word for a fort was included in the new name:

ceaster / **caester** (fort; walled town)

burh / **burg** (fort; fortified place)

Modern English spellings:

-caster   -chester   -cester   -castle

-burgh   -borough   -brough   -berry   -bury

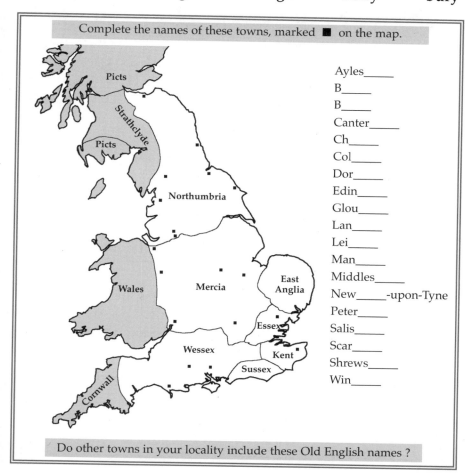

Complete the names of these towns, marked ■ on the map.

Ayles_____
B_____
B_____
Canter_____
Ch_____
Col_____
Dor_____
Edin_____
Glou_____
Lan_____
Lei_____
Man_____
Middles_____
New_____-upon-Tyne
Peter_____
Salis_____
Scar_____
Shrews_____
Win_____

Do other towns in your locality include these Old English names ?

Anglo-Saxon writing

The Anglo-Saxons brought their own writing system with them when they invaded the British Isles. The letters were called **runes**. Like the Celtic oghams *(see p.10)*, they were engraved on stone monuments and also on weapons and armour. Part of an Old English poem, *The Dream of the Rood*, was carved on an 18 foot high cross which can still be seen in the village of Ruthwell, near Dumfries.

The system is called the **futhorc**, after the first few letters:

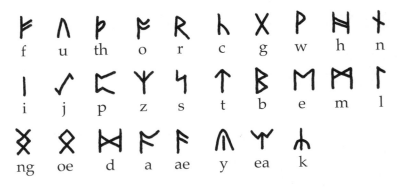

| f | u | th | o | r | c | g | w | h | n |

| i | j | p | z | s | t | b | e | m | l |

| ng | oe | d | a | ae | y | ea | k |

> **i.** Write your name and address in runes.
>
> **ii.** Write the days of the week in runes.

Both the Celts and the Anglo-Saxons had seen the Roman capital alphabet on public buildings and monuments. Are there any similarities between oghams, runes and the Roman capital letters we also use today ?

---

write

This word comes from the Old English verb **writan** which means: **to scratch runes into bark**.

English, Christianity and Latin

The conversion of the English to Christianity was important to the language in many ways, but most of all because it saw the beginning of the use of both Latin words and the Roman alphabet in English.

Celtic monks from Ireland brought their religion to the north and missionaries from Rome came to the south. By 650, the Christian religion was established throughout the country. From that time right up to today, the Latin language has provided a basis from which thousands of new words and parts of words have been added to English. Along with Greek and French, it has had the greatest influence of all.

With the spread of Christianity, monasteries were established all over England and they became centres of learning respected throughout Europe. Many of them had large libraries and the books the monks produced, especially those from Northumbria, were exported in great quantities. Many of the books were copies of the Bible and other religious works written, of course, in Latin, the international language of the Church.

Much of the monks' time was spent in making copies of these works, using the Roman alphabet in various handwriting styles. Their books were often works of art, beautifully written and illustrated with elaborate decorations in gold leaf and rich colour.

Latin into English

As more and more people were converted, the demand grew for the Bible to be written in English. Bede, the most respected of the Northumbrian monks, produced one of the first translations of St. John's Gospel into English.

It was through such translations that Latin words began to creep into English. Whenever the translator came across a Latin word which had no equivalent in Old English, he used the Latin word instead.

Most of the words were to do with the church and its services, for example:

altar	candle	disciple	hymn	mass
minster	monk	noon	nun	offer	organ
pope	priest	psalm	rule	temple

But the church also had a strong influence on everyday life, and words for clothing, food and household items and education were borrowed from Latin too:

cap	sock	silk	chest	mat
lentil	pear	radish	cook	plant
lily	pine	school	master	verse

The words **educate** and **education** did not come into English from Latin until the 15th century.

What word or words could have been used before that date ? Check your ideas in a dictionary.*

See p.52 for how to look up the origin of a word.

The Anglo-Saxon Chronicle

The Anglo-Saxon Chronicle could, from its title, claim to be the first English newspaper. In fact, it is a record of events in Britain covering about 700 years - from the arrival of the Angles, Saxons and Jutes in 449 through to about 1150 - well after the last great invasion of Britain by the French.

King Alfred the Great ordered it to be written towards the end of the 9th century and it was continued by many different scribes for almost 300 years after his death in 899.

Together with the history of the English people written by Bede in 731, it is one of the most important sources of information about the early history of England.

Below is an extract from *The Anglo-Saxon Chronicle* which records the first raids of the Vikings on the British Isles.

789 **In this year King Beorhtric married Offa's daughter Eadburh.**

 **And in his days there came for the first time three ships of Northmen and then the reeve rode to them and wished to force them to the king's residence, for he did not know what they were. And they slew him.**

Those were the first ships of Danish men which came to the land of the English.

The Vikings

The Vikings were from Scandinavia - Danes and Norwegians who, from 789 onwards, raided most parts of the British Isles. After much savage fighting, they eventually settled down to live alongside the English.

Their language, **Old Norse**, had the same Germanic roots as English so, over the years, the two languages mixed quite well. A good example of the likeness between Old English and Old Norse is the name **Viking** itself:

Old Norse	**vik**	=	a bay; inlet
	viking	=	one who knows well the inlets of the sea; seafarer; pirate
Old English	**wic**	=	a camp
	wicing	=	one who makes camp; a pirate

The difference in meaning clearly depends on which side of the fence you live !

Scandinavian place-names

It is easy for the modern reader to see (as in the case of the Anglo-Saxons) the influence of Old Norse in place-names. Some of the most common are:

thorpe	=	farm; small village
stoke	=	place; holy place; monastery
thwaite	=	meadow; fenced-off piece of land
toft	=	site of a house and out-buildings
by	=	village; homestead

Although these names show up Viking settlements almost everywhere in the British Isles, the vast majority of them are found north and east of a line which stretches (roughly) between London and Chester. This area was established, after fierce fighting between English and Vikings, as a kingdom under Danish rule called **Danelaw**.

Map showing Viking settlements in England

The dots mark the many other places with Viking names.

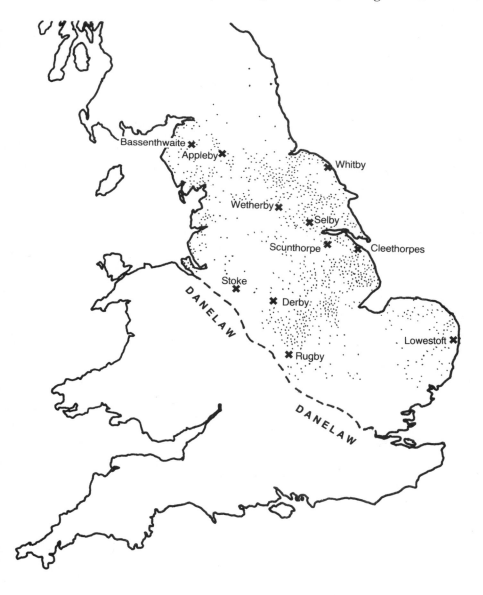

The Calendar - then and now

Days of the week

The days of the week were named by the Anglo-Saxons after the gods and the planets they worshipped before they were converted to Christianity.

Comparing the Old English words with the modern ones shows how, over a period of about 1000 years, slurred speech and changes in the letters representing certain sounds have affected the spellings.

Fill in the Modern English spellings:

ModE	OE	
	Monandaeg	day of the moon
	Tiwesdaeg	day of Tiw - god of war and the sky
	Wodnesdaeg	day of Woden - god of war, wisdom and poetry
	Thunresdaeg	day of Thunor - god of thunder, sky and weather
	Frigesdaeg	day of Frig - goddess of love and fertility
	Saternesdaeg	day of the planet Saturn
	Sunnandaeg	day of the sun

Today, the days of the week are just names - their original significance has gone. The same is true of:

ModE	OE	
holiday	**haligdaeg**	a holy day

Yet, remembering the original meaning of the word might prevent the common spelling mistake - **hoilday** !

Months of the year

There have been many different ways of dividing the year and naming the months. Here are the Old English and Modern English ones (**Note:** The Anglo-Saxon year began on December 25th).

OE		ModE
Giuli	Yuletide - start of the New Year	**December**
Solmonath	month of cakes (offered to the gods)	**January**
Hrethmonath	month of the goddess Hretha	**February**
Eosturmonath	month of the goddess Eostre	**March**
Thrimilci	month when cows were milked three times a day	**April**
Litha	means moon	**May & June**
Weodmonath	month of weeds	**July**
Haligmonath	holy month - the month of offerings (i.e. Harvest)	**August**
Wintirfyllith	first full moon of winter	**September**
Blotmonath	month of sacrifice (blood) - animals killed for food	**October**
Giuli	Yuletide	**November**

There is no obvious link between the Old English and the Modern English names (except that **Eosturmonath** may be the origin of **Easter**).

---

i. Where did the modern names for the months come from ?
   (A standard English dictionary should provide the answer.)

ii. When did January become the first month of the year in England ?
   *(**Whitaker's Almanack** will help here.)*

French ivory carving (10th Century)

English - Ancient and Modern

Here are some examples of the same piece of writing at different stages in the development of English.

Old English - 990

þu ure faeder · þe eart on heoronum · sy ðin
nama gehalgod · Cume ðin rice · Sy ðin
wylla on eorðan swaswa on heoronum · Syle
us todaeg urne daeghwamlican hlaf · And
forgyf us ure gyltas swaswa we forgyraið
ðampe wið us agyltað · And ne laed ðu
na us on costnunge · ac alys us fram yfele ·

Old English (550 - 1100) may, at first glance, look like a foreign language, but many of the most common English words were in use over a thousand years ago and they have remained the same, or only slightly altered, right up to the present day. How many words can you recognise ? *(The Key to translation on p.25 may help.)*

Middle English - 1380

Oure fadir þat art in heuenys. halewid
be þi name. þi kyngdom come to. be þi
wille don as in heuene and in erþe
give to us þis day oure breed ouer
oþer substaunse. and forgiue to us
oure dettes. as and we forgiuen to
oure dettouris. and leede us not
into temptacioun. but delyuere
us from yuel.

Middle English (1100 - 1500) is a halfway stage, in which new words were added to English and spellings changed. Most of the changes came from France because England was under French rule for much of this period. More of the words should be recognisable now. Have you guessed yet what the piece of writing is ?

Modern English - 1611

> **Our Father which art in heaven, Hallowed be thy name. Thy kingdom come. Thy will be done in earth as it is in heaven. Give us this day our daily bread. And forgive us our debts, as we forgive our debtors. And lead us not into temptation, but deliver us from evil.**

Modern English (1500 - present day) had begun to take shape at the beginning of the 16th century. You will now recognise the Lord's Prayer. It is taken from the English version of the Bible authorised by King James I. It has remained in use until the present day and is one of the great works of English literature. About 92% of the words in the Authorised Version of the Bible are Old English words. Although its style is old-fashioned, it is written in words which modern readers know and understand.

Very Modern English - 1989

> **Our Father in heaven, may your name be hallowed; your kingdom come, your will be done, on earth as in heaven. Give us today our daily bread. Forgive us the wrong we have done, as we have forgiven those who have wronged us. And do not put us to the test, but save us from the evil one.**

This version of the Lord's Prayer is to be found in **The Revised English Bible (1989)**. It is a revision of *The New English Bible*, which was published in 1961 as an alternative to the Authorised Version, in the belief that people in the 20th century needed a Bible in more up-to-date English. *The New English Bible* was strongly criticised by many for its stilted language and a lack of any of the qualities of good writing. The revised version seems to have made little improvement. Only time can tell how long it will survive in the ever-changing English language of the next few centuries.

A spot of translating

Despite the many words brought into English from other languages, at least 65% of the words used in everyday speech and writing today are native English words. Some of them have survived the 1200 or so years from Old English with their spelling and pronunciation unchanged. Others have changed slightly, but it only requires a little knowledge and a bit of guesswork to work out their modern spelling.

On the next few pages there are examples of some common words to 'translate' from Old English (OE) into Modern English (ModE).

The key below should help to make most words look more like Modern English. But, first, try to work out the words without it.

Always say the words aloud - trying out different pronunciations may give answers.

Try changing the vowels round too, because their sounds, and the letters representing them, have changed many times over the years.

KEY

OE		ModE
ae	=	a
sc	=	sh
final -g	=	y
final -an	=	ignore it !
c	=	k
hw	=	wh
-ht	=	-ght
cw	=	qu
þ / ð	=	th

Key words

Most of the 100 key words which make up about half of our everyday speech are Old English. Some are still spelt the same way:

and   **for**   **of**   **in**   **to**   **under**   **on**

Others have changed their spelling a little.

Here are 10 common words as they were written about 1300 years ago. Write the Modern English word alongside:

	Old English	Modern English
1.	**aefter**	
2.	**beforan**	
3.	**behindan**	
4.	**bi**	
5.	**eall**	
6.	**hwaet ?**	
7.	**hwy ?**	
8.	**ofer**	
9.	**uppan**	
10.	**aet**	

Clothes

Most of the modern names for clothes are not found in Old English, except for some very basic items.

Guess what these were, and check in a dictionary to see if you were right:

socc   **scoh**   **scyrte**   **haett**

The Family

All the words for our close family come from Old English.

Put the Modern English spelling alongside the Old English one:

Old English	Modern English
faeder	
moder	
sunu	
dohtor	
sweoster	
brothor	

What about our more distant relations ?

Look up the origin of these words in a standard dictionary:

aunt	**uncle**	**niece**	**nephew**
grandfather	**grandmother**		**cousin**

Food and drink

Here are ten basic items of food and drink in Old English.
What is their Modern English spelling ?

OE	ModE	OE	ModE
bread		**cese**	
butere		**mete**	
milc		**aeg**	
sealt		**fisc**	
hunig		**beor**	

Parts of the body

Label the parts of the body, as shown by the lines, using the Old English words given below:

lippe	eare	finger	cneo
haer	hand	fot	heafod
breost	nosu	earm	heorte
scanca *(clue:* Shanks's pony)			

Numbers

Match the Old English words to the figures and write the Modern English spelling alongside:

	Old English	Modern English
1.		
2.		
3.		
4.		
5.		
6.		
7.		
8.		
9.		
10.		

an	**nigon**	**feower**	**siex**	**tyn**
fif	**eahta**	**twa**	**seofon**	**thri**

Roman numerals

The figures 1-10 above are from the Arabic system of writing numbers, which is the one used for most purposes in the U.K.

The other well-known numbering system, often seen on clock and watch faces, is the Roman one which is based on the fingers:

I = one finger   **II** = two fingers

V = the shape made by the thumb and first finger

X = the fingers crossed etc.

Look up a table of Roman numerals in an encyclopaedia and try out all the figures on your hands. Why do you think this system is not used for all mathematical work now ?

The Normans *(The French Connection)*

In 1066, William, Duke of Normandy, defeated Harold Godwinson, King of England, at the Battle of Hastings, and changed the face of the English language. For the next 200 years the French ruled England. The English upper classes were wiped out and replaced by French barons. In the churches and monasteries, Frenchmen took over from English bishops and abbots.

Because those in power spoke only French, it became a sign of social standing to be able to speak French and a vast language division arose between people in the upper classes, who spoke French, and those in the lower classes (the majority) who spoke only English.

In the years between 1066 and 1500, over 10,000 words came into English from French, and for almost 200 of those years there was so little writing in English that many native English people almost forgot how to read it. Latin, the language of the church, was used as a common language when the English and their French rulers could not understand each other.

Scholars call the language of this time **Middle English** because of the many changes in both spoken and written English which took place. By 1500, to the eyes of a modern reader, English was beginning to look less like a foreign language and more like the English of today.

---

qu

After the Conquest, French scribes started to bring French letter patterns into English - 'qu' was one of them.

The Old English spelling of this sound was 'cw', as in cwic, cwen and cwell, but the French had always used the Latin letters for it and so we now have **quick**, **queen** and **quell**.

---

wh

This letter pattern started life the other way round. It was written 'hw' in Old English, because the 'h' was always spoken.

French scribes, however, decided to tidy things up a bit. 'th' was already used in English, so the French added 'ch' to go with it, and then they changed 'hw' to 'wh' to follow the same pattern. It has stayed this way ever since.

Some people today (especially in Scotland and Ireland) still carefully pronounce the 'h' sound as well as the 'w' in words which begin with 'wh'.

Give the Modern English spelling of these words:		
Old English		*Modern English*
hwaer	=	where
hwaenne	=	when
hwil	=	
hwaet	=	
hwi (or **hwy**)	=	
hwaether	=	
hwilc	=	

With some words the scribes got a bit carried away and added 'w' to words which had previously only begun with 'h'. This is why we are now saddled with **whole** (**hal** in Old English) and **whore** (**hore** in Old English).

The final oddity in this group is:

    (Old English) **hwa** = **who** *(Modern English)*

in which we now manage to pronounce the 'h' and miss out the 'w' sound altogether !

French into English

One of the first words to come into English from French after the Conquest was **peace**. Was it a command (or could it have been a request ?) from the French to the stubborn English they were trying to rule ?

As might be expected, many of the words to do with the interests of the ruling classes - government, the law, the church, the arts - came into English from French:

parliament	mayor	tax	city	county
army	navy	soldier	battle	captain
crime	justice	jury	arrest	prison	constable
baptise	bible	vicar	saint	sermon
music	poetry	comedy	fashion	luxury	satin

Although some French words replaced English ones, many were added alongside them, giving us new ways of expressing ourselves, for example:

English:	book	tongue	smell	sorrow	ask
French:	volume	language	scent	grief	question

A book called *A Speller's Companion* could not have been written before 1200, because the only word in the title which existed in English was 'A' and it was written 'An'.

The Anglo-Saxons did not 'spell' as we do today, and they had 'friends' but not 'companions' until the French introduced the words.

Perhaps an Old English edition of the book might have been entitled *An Word-handleres Freond*.

French and food

The French have provided us with both basic and fancy names for food and for the places in which we eat it.

Is there an alternative English word for any of these and, if there is, how often is it used ?

café	beef	saucer
restaurant	pork	dinner
menu	mutton	dine
à la carte	rabbit	quiche
table d'hôte	sausage	vol-au-vent
hors d'oeuvre	pâté	casserole
entrée	tart	picnic
sauce	gâteau	pâtisserie
pie	dessert	créme de menthe

French at random

This list of English words with French origins was made from an idle browse through a dictionary:

garage	cul-de-sac	blouse
petrol	chimney	dress
souvenir	avenue	frock
R.S.V.P.	passage	embroidery
au revoir	passport	toilet
moustache	palace	lingerie

Try it yourself and see what you come up with.

The origins of writing

The need for a system of writing language down only arose when primitive nomadic people began to settle down to live in one place, farm the land and organise themselves as a community. They then needed to keep records of their property, the goods they traded, their religious practices, and the way they ran their community.

The earliest examples of writing come from the Middle East and most of the development of writing systems into the alphabets used today took place in the countries around the Mediterranean in the 3000 years before the birth of Christ.

Writing systems went through several stages which can be divided, roughly, as follows:

Pictograms

The simplest form of keeping records was to paint or engrave pictures on walls, on stone or in wet clay:

$$\text{🦆} = \text{bird} \qquad \text{🦆🦆} = \text{2 birds}$$

$$\text{🐂} = \text{ox} \qquad \text{🐂🐂🐂} = \text{3 oxen}$$

Ideograms

The use of pictures was then extended so that a picture could represent both an object and abstract ideas connected with it:

$$\bigodot = \textbf{sun} \; or \; \textbf{day} \; or \; \textbf{time}$$

The ideogram is still used today in Chinese writing and also in many international symbols, which can be understood regardless of the language people speak:

What do the above ideograms mean ?

Phonograms

Next came the idea of using a picture to represent a sound, and two or more pictures could be put together to make a word:

🐝 = bee + 🍃 = leaf makes 🐝 🍃 = belief

Symbols

The phonogram led on to the invention of a series of symbols, based on pictures, each of which represented a single sound - often that of the first letter of the original word picture:

🖘 = A (**aleph** was the Hebrew word for **ox**)

This style of writing was called **cuneiform** and it was done with a triangle-shaped tool pressed into a tablet of wet clay. The clay was then left to harden for storing.

The Egyptians used both pictures and symbols for words and sounds in their **hieroglyphic** writing system. They created 24 symbols to represent consonant sounds:

e.g.   O = h   ⌐⊐ = b   ☐ = p   ⬭ = r

The Greeks added extra symbols to the Egyptian ones, mainly for vowel sounds, and called their writing system the **alphabet**, after the first two letters, *alpha* and *beta*. From them it passed to the Romans and then, gradually, it spread throughout Europe and to much of the East. In each language in which it was used, the alphabet was adapted to fit its own particular speech sounds. On the next page is a table showing how some of the letters have ended up in different languages.

The symbols for sounds have moved so far away from the original pictures they were based on that there is no obvious link between them. The letters of the alphabet are 'eye signs' which can be recognised by people of many different languages - just as the mathematical signs and figures below are internationally understood:

2   5   7   =   %   +   ÷   £ $ €

The alphabet in different languages

The table below shows some of the letters of the alphabet written in different languages. Note how similar letter shapes settled down in various scripts. At first, there was no fixed order in writing and, even when it did get organised into lines, they could start from left or right, or top or bottom.

Early Greek & Roman	Ogham	Runic	Later Roman	Later Greek	Russian
			A	Α	А
			B	Β	Б
			D	Δ	Д
			E	Ε	Е
			L	Λ	Л
			M	Μ	М
	none		P	Ρ	П
			T	Τ	Т

Early writing materials and letter shapes

The writing material used for the early developments of the alphabet often dictated the shapes of letters.

Cuneiform letters were wedge-shaped because they were made by jabbing a stick into wet clay. The Egyptian **hieroglyphs** were written with a **reed brush** on smooth **papyrus** (also made from reeds) and curved letter shapes were easily produced.

Roman and Greek **capital letters** were engraved in **stone** and the shape of the **chisel** they used made straight lines easy and curves difficult. This may explain why the Romans used **V** for **U** in their capital alphabet. For everyday writing they used a **reed pen** and **papyrus**, or an **iron stylus** and a **tablet** filled with **soft wax**. With these their letters could become flowing and rounded.

36

Early writing materials and their uses

The two stories below describe practices which are still carried on, in slightly different ways, today.

In Greece, broken pieces of unglazed pottery, called **ostraca**, were used for writing short notes or lists.

In Athens, secret ballots were held now and then, in which all citizens could give the names of people in the city they thought to be too powerful or dangerous. The names were written on **ostraca** and put in a large urn. Anyone who received too many votes was **ostracised** - that is, he was banished from Athens for at least ten years.

Today, the physical punishment may not be so severe, but the experience of **ostracism** is not a pleasant one.

In England, in the Middle Ages, **parchment** (made from animal skins) and **quill pens** (made from the wing feathers of birds) were used for writing.

It was well known that the hair side of the parchment was the best side and would stand up well to the correcting of errors. The flesh side, however, was lighter in colour and the surface came up very rough and furry if any attempt at rubbing out was made.

Treasury officials, therefore, always ordered cheap parchment, and insisted that only the flesh side should be used for the accounts, so that any errors or attempts at embezzlement could be spotted immediately !

Word origins to do with writing

alphabet

The name used for the letters in the English writing system comes from Greek. It is based on their names for the first two letters - **alpha (A)** and **beta (B)**. It is thought that the alphabet is in a particular order because the Greeks and the Hebrews used it as a counting system too:

$$A = 1 \qquad B = 2 \qquad C = 3 \quad etc.$$

The Romans brought the alphabet to the British Isles, and they had several different versions of it which they used for different purposes:

THE CAPITAL ALPHABET
(*Latin:* **capitalis** = chief; head)

There were two sets of capital letters:

CAPITALIS MONUMENTALIS: the most important alphabet, with large, elegant letters, used (as its name suggests) for carving inscriptions on public buildings or for public notices painted on walls.

CAPITALIS RUSTICA: a narrower form of capital alphabet used for the same official purposes.

The cursive alphabet
(*Latin:* **currere** = to run)

The cursive alphabet was used for everyday writing. The word means, literally, **flowing, running** or **quickly written**. It was based on the capital letters, but it could be written in a large size (**majuscule**) or a smaller size (**minuscule**) which had letters joined by loops above and below the line.

This alphabet was used, in many different styles, over a period of about 1400 years, for writing books and official documents. It was often referred to as a 'book hand'.

Scribal errors ?

Some of the oddities of English spelling can be laid at the door of those who put the language into written form. From the time when people began to write down their speech, to the invention of the printing press in Germany in 1440, all books and official documents were written entirely by hand.

Monks and nuns

The earliest scribes in England were monks and nuns, who were used to copying religious texts - mainly in Latin. As people were converted to Christianity, the monasteries became centres of learning and education and the demand for their books increased all over Europe.

In England, people wanted the Bible and other works to be written in English, not Latin. This created new work and new problems for the monks who had to translate from Latin into English.

For example, if there was no existing word in English to use for a Latin one, either a new word had to be invented or the Latin word had to be brought into English use.

Often, the letters of the Roman alphabet did not quite fit English speech sounds and letters had to be combined in new patterns. Sometimes, old letters whose sound was no longer in use were brought back again to represent a new sound.

There was also the more practical problem of how to fit the writing neatly into a page. Since there was no standard spelling for most English words at that time, letters were often added or left out at random, just to make a line fit between the margins.

In some handwriting styles, certain letters were hard to read alongside other letters with similar shapes. The monks had an answer for this. It is described on the next page.

'Money' worries

One of the most common queries today is why words like **money** and **honey** and **some** and **wonder** should be spelt with an '**o**', when the letter sounds like '**u**'.

In both Latin and French, '**o**' had replaced '**u**' in words where it was placed next to '**n**' or '**m**' or '**v**' or '**w**' (which was written '**uu**' then, as its name suggests), because its round shape stood out between the vertical lines of the other letters and made it much easier to read. So the monks began to use the same method when writing in English. That is why we now have spellings like:

monk   **come**   **worry**   **love**   **above**   **son**   **tongue**

It was a simple and practical solution. But, as usual, not all words fitted conveniently into the pattern.

Some Old English words like **Monday**, **month** and **mother** were spoken with a long '**o**' sound in them (as in m**oa**n). It is thought that, in these words, it was simply due to a gradual change in pronunciation that the '**o**' sound was slurred into the short '**u**' sound used today.

Professional scribes

Although the monasteries had the monopoly of book production until the 12th century, they had, for a long time, taken in apprentices to work alongside them and learn their skills. As the demand for books grew, these 'lay' scribes (or **scriveners**) set up their own workshops and, along with the other craftsmen involved in the making of books - illuminators, parchmenters and bookbinders - they formed guilds (trade unions) to protect themselves against unfair competition. They began to provide books and documents for a growing market among the richer trades-people and the students at the new universities appearing all over Europe.

A trick of the trade

The professional scribes, when making books, came across exactly the same problems as the monks had and they dealt with them in the same individual way. But there was one big difference between them - the monks did their work for the glory of God, while the laymen did it to earn a living.

Right up to the end of the 16th century, scriveners charged for their work by the inch. During that century, it was fashionable among writers to show off their learning by using long Latin words. Crafty scriveners took advantage of this and often replaced an English word with a longer Latin one in order to add to their income.

This practice brought them a rather pompous rebuke from Richard Mulcaster, one of the earliest spelling reformers:

> *'If words be ouercharged with number of letters,*
> *that coms either by couetousnesse in such as sell*
> *them by lines, or by ignorance.'*

---

scribe   **script**   **scrivener**

1. Look up the origin of these words in a standard dictionary.

2. The first two, as well as being words in their own right, form either the root or a part of many English words. List some of them, look up their meanings and notice how the root word fits into the meaning of the new word.

Word origins to do with scribes

Some words in common use today come from the time when books were handwritten:

---

stationer

(*Latin:* **statio** = a standing still, station; post)

A stationer, in the Middle Ages, was a bookseller who 'stayed in one place' and acted as middleman between customers and craftsmen. He took orders for books to be made, co-ordinated the work of the different craftsmen, supplied their materials and also commissioned new books to be sold, ready-made, in his shop.

In addition, he often ran a hire service for students who could not afford to buy books. They hired them instead and took them home to copy out overnight.

masterpiece

During the last year of his apprenticeship in a workshop, a young scribe had to prepare an example of his best work to present to the masters of his guild. If this **masterpiece** was considered good enough, he became a qualified 'journeyman' scribe. This meant that he now had to spend some time away from the security of the workshop as a freelance scribe, until he had gained enough experience and money to open his own workshop.

red-letter day

Mediaeval books and documents often contained small headings or initial letters written in red and known as **rubrics** (*Latin:* **rubor** = red). These rubrics marked important sections of the text.

In calendars, at that time, the saints' days were always highlighted in this way, and that is why a special or important day has come to be called a **red-letter** day.

Speech *v.* writing

Speech is affected most by the places where people live and those with whom they come into contact every day. Because English is a mixture of several languages, and also has many dialects within those languages, there is great variety both in the way people pronounce words and in the words they use for the same thing.

Pronunciation

Everyone knows about the North/South division in England over the pronunciation of **bath** (and words like it). If it were written as spoken, it could be:

bath (North)   **barth** (South)   **beth** (posh)

Also, within the U.K., some spellings of **first** could be:

forst (Newcastle)   **fairst** (Liverpool)   **furst** (S. Wales)

fearst (Scotland)   **farst** (posh)

The modern 'luxury' of a standard spelling for each word, regardless of how it is spoken, was not available to most people until the 18th century. Before that, they spelled as they spoke.

Most spelling problems today can be put down to the simple fact that the pronunciation of letters and words has changed many times in the history of English, and is still changing, whilst the written letters and words have remained unchanged.

Vowel sounds have been the main victims of change. During the 15th century, a complete change took place in the way long vowel sounds were pronounced. Scholars call it the **Great Vowel Shift**. Some consonants which were once pronounced are now silent; others now have different letters to represent them. Several spellings have been deliberately altered by poets to make rhyming words look, as well as sound, the same.

And the scribes and printers responsible for presenting the chaos of spoken English in written form all found their own solutions - and increased the confusion !

was

The pronunciation of **was** is a good example of how the spoken and written versions of a word have gone their separate ways.

As London grew in size and power, its citizens developed what they regarded as a more refined form of speech. It is thought that they did it partly to distinguish themselves from the rough-and-ready 'provincials' with their broad vowels and blunt speech.

It may be due to them that words like **was**, **wander** and **watch** - all good Old English words in which 'a' was pronounced as in **has** or **hat** - began to be spoken with the mouth almost closed, so that 'a' sounded more like 'o' or 'u'. Unfortunately for us, they left the spelling alone and it has stayed **was** ever since.

Experts in spoken language also claim that it is difficult to say short 'a' (as in **has**) when it is next to 'w' (as in **was**) - but the Anglo-Saxons seemed to manage it all right (and so do Northumbrians today !).

Different words for the same thing

The mixture of languages and dialects in the British Isles caused some problems for the early printers, but it is this very mixture that makes the English language so rich and varied.

Here are some of the words used in the British Isles for a **bread roll**:

barm	**bap**	**batch**	**bun**
breadie	**cob**	**bridge roll**	

What word do you use for these ?

left-handed   **Autumn**   **friend**   **little**

a tiny piece of wood stuck in your finger

gh

Many spelling problems are caused by letters which appear in a word but are no longer pronounced. The history of '**gh**' is a good example.

When Old English scribes began writing the language down, they could find no letter, in the alphabets they knew, which represented the hard breathing sound (a bit like '**ch**' in the Scots word **loch**) which was heard in many Old English words. So they chose the letter '**h**'.

Most of the words which now have '**gh**' in them were spelt in Old English just with '**h**' - and the '**h**' was pronounced, like the '**ch**' in **loch**:

Old English: **niht**   **riht**   **miht**   **boht**   **thoht**

For several hundred years, this spelling and the way it was spoken remained the same.

Then, during the 15th century, a '**g**' was added to the '**h**' to make '**gh**', and that spelling has survived up to the present day:

Modern English: **night**   **right**   **might**   **bought**   **thought**

But - by the time of Shakespeare and Queen Elizabeth 1 (about 100 years later), people had stopped pronouncing the '**gh**' sound altogether ! So, for the last 400 years we have, perversely, continued to write two letters, in certain words, which we no longer use in speech.

In 1476, William Caxton set up the first English printing press and added to the confusion. Caxton had trained as a printer in Holland, where they used '**gh**' to represent the hard '**g**' sound. Caxton decided to do the same in some English words, so he changed the Old English words **gost**, **gastly** and **gerkin** to **ghost**, **ghastly** and **gherkin**.

And that is not quite the end of the '**gh**' story. Other printers, searching for a symbol to use for the '**f**' sound in certain words, came up with - you've guessed it - '**gh**' ! Now you know why we have **laugh** and **cough** and **tough** and **rough**.

More silent letters

Of the 26 letters of the alphabet only 5 are never silent in English. They are **F**, **J**, **Q**, **V** and **X**. The other 21, at some time or another, can be silent. Some 'silent' letters crop up so often that it is worth trying to find out why they are there at all.

1. **k** *(in **kn**)*;   **w** *(in **wr**)*

   These letters were once pronounced. Read out these two lists of words, pronouncing the first letter:

   know   **k**not   **k**nock   **k**nit   **k**nife   **k**nee   **k**nuckle   **k**nob

   write   **w**rong   **w**ren   **w**restle   **w**rinkle   **w**rist

   It is clear that a sentence with several of these words in it soon becomes a tongue-twister and so the first letter has gradually disappeared from speech.

   Unfortunately, it has not disappeared from writing. In some words this is useful because the silent letter can show the difference in spelling between two words with the same sound but a different meaning:

   write / rite   **k**not / not

2. final '**e**'

   In the 16th century, Richard Mulcaster, a schoolmaster and scholar who wrote one of the earliest books on spelling, suggested that the letter '**e**' should be added to words of one syllable containing a vowel, as a way of showing readers that the vowel should be spoken as a long one (*e.g.* **mad** / **made**; **bit** / **bite**). It was a good idea and it is still in use today.

   But, as with most things in English, it was used rather too freely by some printers and many words were given a final '**e**' when they didn't fit the rule. This probably explains the modern spelling and pronunciation of words like:

   some   **gone**   **done**   **give**   **love**   **have**

3. **p** (*as in **pneumonia** or **psychology**);*   **m** (*as in **mnemonic***)

All of these letter patterns are from Greek. From the 16th century onwards, words from Greek and Latin have been brought into English, mainly by scientists and scholars, to give names to new discoveries and inventions - especially in the field of medicine. The Greek or Latin spelling has been kept, when written, to show the origin of the word but, in speech, the first letter was soon dropped because it was awkward to say.

4. **b**

Writers in the 16th century, attempting to show off their knowledge of Latin, have caused unnecessary problems in spelling by adding letters to existing English words to make them look more like the Latin word:

dette (*Middle English*) became **debt** (*Latin:* **debitum**)

doute (*Middle English*) became **doubt** (*Latin:* **dubitare**)

5. **could / would / should**

There seems to have been a lot of confusion over these words. This is what is known:

In Old English: **wolde** = would

                scyld = should

                cuthe = could

The letter 'l' was sounded in Old English; 'sc' was pronounced 'sh'; 'y' was pronounced almost as 'ou' is in the modern spelling.

By the 16th century, **should** and **would** were spelt as they are today. Presumably their vowel sounds and the spellings of them had merged to arrive at the present pronunciation, and the 'l' sound had disappeared. Then, it seems, some writer decided to change **cuthe** to **could** so that all three words might look and sound the same. Eureka ! (*Greek:* I have found)

Caxton and printing

The first English printing press was set up by William Caxton in 1476 and, some say, set back the standardisation of spelling some 50 years !

Despite the many problems involved in the writing of English, the professional scriveners of the past 400 years had worked towards a standard form of spelling and had, in many ways, achieved it. Caxton had been abroad for many years, training to be a printer, and he was out of touch with developments in English spelling.

Caxton was, above all, a businessman - and a successful one, too; but he used foreign machinery and employed foreign printers who had even less knowledge of English spelling than their boss had. Caxton's own blunder in bringing the '**gh**' spelling pattern from Holland is dealt with elsewhere in this book, but he was also careless about checking the work of his employees and the books they produced were full of inconsistent spellings.

The one advantage of the earliest printing presses was that they could produce copies of books much more quickly. In all other respects, the handwritten books of the scriveners were far better.

What Caxton did do, however, was to print all his books in just one of the many dialects of the British Isles. In the interests of business, he had to choose the one which could be read and understood by most people. He chose the dialect of the East Midlands, which was spoken by most people in the eastern half of England from the River Humber to the River Thames. This area included London, where Caxton had his business. Other printers followed Caxton's lead, and the speech of London and the area around it became the basis of Standard English as we now know it.

It is interesting to consider that, if Caxton's press had been set up in Edinburgh, Standard English might well have been Scots or Northumbrian, since those dialects were spoken by as many, if not more, people.

Printers' errors

Although the early printers did try to use a standard form of spelling, they also continued, for several hundred years, to take advantage of the confusion about 'correct' spelling when it was more practical for them to do so.

For example, when trying to 'justify' a line of print (*i.e.* to make it fit between straight left and right margins), they would add or omit letters at random, giving alternatives like:

dog   **dogg**   **dogge**

been   **beene**   **bin**

fellow   **felow**   **felowe**   **fallow**   **fallowe**

It was quite common to have several different spellings of a word on the same page.

It was only when the first widely used dictionary was published, in 1755, that printers really had a standard work to refer to when in doubt about the spelling of a word.

---

upper case and lower case

These two terms, used to describe the size of letters, come from printers.

Printers kept sets of the letter blocks they used for printing in a case with two compartments. The upper compartment held the capital letters and the lower one held the small ones.

Dictionaries

Present-day writers turn to the dictionary automatically to check both spellings and meanings of words. It is taken for granted. And yet, out of the 1300 or so years of written English, it is only in the last 250 years that it has been possible for most people in the British Isles to obtain one.

Since 1066, when the French opened the flood-gates, thousands of new words have poured into English from all over the world.

It is said that Shakespeare had the largest vocabulary of any writer ever, and often invented his own words if necessary. These words were used for the first time in English by Shakespeare:

accommodation   **apostrophe**   **assassination**   **obscene**

The variable spelling of Shakespeare and his printers has founded a huge industry devoted entirely to the study of his writing, how it is spelt and what the words mean.

Until the second half of the 18th century, people spelled, by and large, as they spoke, especially in their own private writing, despite the efforts of scribes, printers, schoolmasters and scholars to establish a standard form of spelling for use throughout England.

Although the idea of spelling words exactly as we like seems very attractive, in practice it makes communication between people very difficult and frustrating. There is a lot to be said for having a standard spelling for each word which can be written and understood by everyone, regardless of the way they say it.

In 1582, Richard Mulcaster, headmaster of Merchant Taylors' School and one of the first writers on the spelling of the English language, wrote:

> *'It were a thing verie praiseworthie in my opinion .... if som one well learned .... wold gather all the words which we use in our English tung .... into one dictionarie.'*

In the following years, many people made the attempt. Some of the most important are described briefly on the next page.

Dictionary landmarks

A Table Alphabeticall (1604) was the first real dictionary of English. It contained about 2500 'hard' words, with brief definitions and was compiled by its author, Robert Cawdrey, 'for the benefit and helpe of Ladies and other unskilfull persons' !

An Universall Etymological English Dictionary (1721) compiled by Nathaniel Bailey, was the first attempt to list and define all the words in the English language. It was regularly revised and reprinted - the 1736 edition contained about 60,000 words - and it had no rival for over 30 years.

A Dictionary of the English Language (1755). Dr. Samuel Johnson, one of the greatest English writers, took seven years to complete the two volumes of his dictionary. Although it contained fewer words than Bailey's (about 40,000), it is regarded as the first important English dictionary because it provided spellings which could be accepted as standard throughout the country, as well as giving fuller definitions of the meanings of words, with examples of the words in use. It was the first dictionary to be bought and widely used in both private homes and public institutions, and it continued in use for over a century with little competition.

The Oxford English Dictionary (1879 onwards) is considered the greatest dictionary of any language in the world. Its first editor, James Murray, a Scotsman, expected that the dictionary would take 10 years to complete. After 5 years, he and his colleagues had only reached the word *'ant'*. It was not until April 1928, 13 years after James Murray's death, that the last of the ten volumes covering the whole alphabet was printed. Several supplements were then added to it, the last of which appeared in 1986.

In 1989, a complete 20-volume 2nd edition was published from a computerised master copy which will make future editions much easier to produce. The 2nd edition is available online and on CD-ROM and, at the time of writing, a 3rd edition is in preparation. The *O.E.D.* contains over 500,000 words. New words come into use daily and the work of updating it never stops.

How to look up a word origin

In all standard dictionaries, the section in square brackets at the end of the entry for each word explains its origin. Here is an entry for 'write', and an explanation of the bracketed section.

write (rart) *vb* writes, writing, wrote, written. 1 to draw or mark (symbols, words, etc.) on a surface, usually paper, with a pen, pencil, or other instrument. 2 to describe or record (ideas, experiences, etc.) in writing. 3 to compose (a letter) to or correspond regularly with (a person, organization, etc.). 4 (*tr; may take a clause as object*) to say or communicate by letter: *he wrote that he was on his way.* 5 (*tr*) *Informal, chiefly U.S. and Canadian.* to send a letter to (a person, etc.). 6 to write (words) in cursive as opposed to printed style. 7 (*tr*) to be sufficiently familiar with (a specified style, language, etc.) to use it in writing. 8 to be the author or composer of (books, music, etc.). 9 (*tr*) to fill in the details for (a document, form, etc.). 10 (*tr*) to draw up or draft. 11 (*tr*) to produce by writing: *he wrote ten pages.* 12 (*tr*) to show clearly: *envy was written all over his face.* 13 (*tr*) to spell, inscribe, or entitle. 14 (*tr*) to ordain or prophesy: *it is written.* 15 (*intr*) to produce writing as specified. 16 *Computing.* to record (data) in a location in a storage device. Compare **read**[1] (sense 16). 17 (*tr*) See **underwrite** (sense 3a). ◆ See also **write down, write in, write off, write out, write up.** [Old English *wrītan* (originally: to scratch runes into bark); related to Old Frisian *wrīta*, Old Norse *rīta*, Old High German *rīzan* (German *reissen* to tear)] ▸ 'writable *adj*

1	3

Old English *writan* (originally: to scratch runes into bark); related to

Old Frisian *writa*, Old Norse *rita*, Old High German *rizan*

(German *reissen* to tear)

1 This is the period when the word was first used in English. This explanation always comes first, in any dictionary. Some dictionaries only give initials (**OE** = Old English). If so, an explanatory list will be given elsewhere in the dictionary.

2 The same word as it is spelt in other old languages of that time. This helps to show the links between languages, many of which belong to the same large Indo European family *(See p.55).*

3 The original meaning of the word and its meaning in a related language show how subtle changes in meaning can take place, and shed new light on words we take for granted.

Using the information given on *p.52*, look for the origins of the word '**spell**', below.

Note that there are three different entries for '**spell**'. Do the various origins and meanings have anything in common ?

spelk (spɛlk) *n Scot. and northern English dialect.* a splinter of wood. [from Old English *spelc, spilc* surgical splint; related to Old Norse *spelkur* splints]

spell[1] (spɛl) *vb* **spells, spelling; spelt** *or* **spelled. 1** to write or name in correct order the letters that comprise the conventionally accepted form of (a word or part of a word). **2** (*tr*) (of letters) to go to make up the conventionally established form of (a word) when arranged correctly: *d-o-g spells dog.* **3** (*tr*) to indicate or signify: *such actions spell disaster for our cause.* ◆ See also **spell out.** [C13: from Old French *espeller*, of Germanic origin; related to Old Norse *spialla* to talk, Middle High German *spellen*] ► '**spellable** *adj*

spell[2] (spɛl) *n* **1** a verbal formula considered as having magical force. **2** any influence that can control the mind or character; fascination. **3** a state induced by or as if by the pronouncing of a spell; trance: *to break the spell.* **4 under a spell.** held in or as if in a spell. ◆ *vb* **5** (*tr*) *Rare.* to place under a spell. [Old English *spell* speech; related to Old Norse *spjall* tale, Gothic *spill*, Old High German *spel*]

spell[3] (spɛl) *n* **1** an indeterminate, usually short, period of time: *a spell of cold weather.* **2** a period or tour of duty after which one person or group relieves another. **3** *Scot., Austral., and N.Z.* a period or interval of rest. ◆ *vb* **4** (*tr*) to take over from (a person) for an interval of time; relieve temporarily. **5 spell a paddock.** *N.Z.* to give a field a rest period by letting it lie fallow. [Old English *spelian* to take the place of, of obscure origin]

Look up the origin of these words:

read   book   word   dictionary   language   origin

1. What is the difference between the first three and the last three words ?

2. What information do these words give about the history of the English language ?

Extracts taken from **Collins English Dictionary**

Miscellany

Which language or country do these words come from ?

tobacco	banana
potato	chocolate
piano	hurricane
yacht	coffee
bungalow	caravan
tea	kitchen
blizzard	tattoo
pyjamas	solo
snack	kangaroo
cinema	kimono
tomato	yoghurt
automatic	camouflage
toboggan	cruise
blitz	catastrophe

What do these words have in common ?

sandwich	cardigan	pasteurise
boycott	diesel	wellington
biro	balaclava	mackintosh

What word do *you* use for the word in bold italics ?
"What's the matter, *pet* ?"

The Indo European languages

The diagram shows the main groups of languages which have grown out of the original Indo European language.

Looking at the similarities between them is interesting in itself, but especially so for anyone going on holiday abroad.

CELTIC	GERMANIC	LATIN	ANCIENT GREEK	SLAVIC	SANSKRIT	IRANIAN
Scots Gaelic	English	Italian	Modern Greek	Russian	Hindi	Persian
Irish Gaelic	German	French		Polish	Urdu	
Welsh	Dutch	Spanish		Czech	Punjabi	
Breton	Flemish	Portugese		Ukrainian	Bengali	
	Swedish	Rumanian		Lithuanian		
	Norwegian			Serbo-Croat		
	Danish					
	Icelandic					

Books for further reading

The books in this list are those which were referred to most often while writing A Speller's Companion. All of them could be classed as 'a good read' as long as they are taken in small doses. Most have an index of some sort, or a fairly detailed list of contents. Some titles are now out of print but they should be available from public libraries.

A History of the English Language by A.C. Baugh and T. Cable
pub. Routledge & Kegan Paul 1951 (5th edition 2002)
The standard work on the history of English. Used, it seems, by every writer on the subject. Divided into short, easily digestible sections.

Language Made Plain by Anthony Burgess
pub. Fontana/Collins 1975 (Paperback)
The author's enthusiasm for language and his wide knowledge of it bring linguistics alive for the ordinary reader.

Language & Communication (Books 1 & 2) by I. Forsyth & K. Wood
pub. Longman 1977 & 1980 (Paperback)
The first two books in a series of three written for secondary schools, which include material on the history of English. Excellent illustrations and clear print make them a pleasure to read. No index.

The Excellency of the English Tongue by F.E. Halliday
pub. Gollancz 1975
A shorter-than-most history of English aimed at the general reader.

The Mother Tongue by Lancelot Hogben
pub. Secker & Warburg 1964
Full of fascinating material on the links between English and other languages. An excellent broad view of what language is about, but frustrating - no index !

The Story of Writing by Donald Jackson
pub. Studio Vista 1981 (also in Paperback, pub. Barrie & Jenkins 1987)
A beautifully illustrated book on the history of how language has been written down from the beginning to the present day.

The Story of English by R. McCrum, W. Cran and R. MacNeil
pub. BBC/Faber and Faber 1986 (also in Paperback 1992)
Written to go with the BBC TV series of the same name. Very good on English as a world language and contains more information about present-day English than most books. Excellent notes at the end include books for further reading.

Language Links by Clive Jenkins
pub. Harrap 1980 (Paperback)
A short book *(48 pages)* on English and its links with other languages, written for schools and colleges. Quite small print. No index.

A History of English Spelling by D.G. Scragg
pub. Manchester University Press 1974
Scholarly, but extremely useful because it deals specifically with the history of spelling.

Dictionaries

Most dictionaries are regularly revised and updated and the latest editions of the titles listed here should be available in hardback or paperback.

Collins English Dictionary
An excellent standard dictionary which has a useful introduction on the pronunciation of English and its development as a world language.

The Concise Oxford Dictionary of English Etymology
Useful for more detail on the origins of words.

The Concise Oxford Dictionary of English Place-names
Very good, but what a pity it hasn't got Wales, Scotland and Ireland too ! There are other works to cover these and many books on place-names in individual counties and regions.

Other publications

*Since **A Speller's Companion** was first published, other books on the English language have appeared. These ones are entertaining and informative, include an index and are well worth dipping into.*

The Adventure of English by Melvyn Bragg
pub. Hodder & Stoughton 2003 (also in Paperback 2004)

A Mouthful of Air by Anthony Burgess
pub. Hutchinson 1992 (also in Paperback, pub. Vintage 1993)

Mother Tongue: The English Language by Bill Bryson
pub. Hamish Hamilton 1990 (also in Paperback, pub. Penguin Books 1991)

The Cambridge Encyclopedia of the English Language by David Crystal
pub. Cambridge University Press 1995 (2nd edition 2003, Hardback & Paperback)

Subject Index

Page numbers of subjects are given for their main entries in the book.

Exercises are interspersed with the text and can be found in shaded boxes like this one, on the following pages:

8, 9, 10, 13, 14, 16, 20, 21, 25, 26, 27, 28, 29, 31, 33, 41, 44, 53, 54

Word Index

Words and spelling patterns listed here are discussed in the book on the pages given. Words from Latin (p.16) and French (pp.32/33) are not listed again here.

Greetings cards / Notelets

A pack of 4 designs based on extracts from *A Speller's Companion*, which show Runes; Oghams; Days - then and now; Months - then and now. Blank for your own message, they are printed in brown on the same cream recycled card as the cover of the book.

Pack with envelopes *(inc. VAT & postage)*: **£1.50**
Available from Brown and Brown *(address overleaf)*.

Other books on spelling and language

Crosswords for Photocopying: Books 1 - 4   *64 pages each*
A set of crossword books for adults who are improving their spelling. Straightforward, non-cryptic clues.

Everyday Spelling   *64 pages*
A workbook providing practice in some of the basics of spelling and writing.

Looking at Spelling *(Photocopy Master)*   *48 pages   A4*
A book of worksheets for photocopying, providing practice in the recognition and use of 2-letter spelling patterns.

Phrases   *64 pages*
A book of exercises on popular English catch phrases, clichés and proverbs, including information on their origins.

Spelling Worksheets *(Photocopy Master)*   *48 pages   A4*
A book of worksheets for photocopying, covering a wide range of spelling and writing topics.

Use your eyes   *56 pages*
A book of enjoyable exercises for improving the visual memory which is the key to good spelling.

Word Play   *64 pages*
A book of 40 word games for adults and children, most of which can be played with pencil and paper or a set of letters.

For a complete catalogue of publications, please contact:
Brown and Brown Publishing, Keeper's Cottage, Westward, Wigton, Cumbria CA7 8NQ   Tel. 016973 42915